DO-IT-YOURSELF GUIDES

The Essential Workshop

Quality tools to build your world.

ACKNOWLEDGEMENTS

Created by Creative Publishing international
in conjunction with WSP Marketing International Ltd.,
47 Valleybrook Drive, Don Mills, Ontario M3B 2S6,
Canada.

**Creative Publishing international
Book Development Staff**

Vikki Anderson
Shawn Binkowski
Steve Boman
Janice Cauley
Marcia Chambers
Maren Christensen
Paul Currie
Doug Deutscher
Melissa Erickson
Jacque Fletcher
John Fletcher
Brad Kissell
Janet Lawrence
Bill Nelson
Chuck Nields
Jon Simpson
Greg Wallace
Gina Wornson

Printed on Canadian paper by World Color
Book Services, USA.

ISBN 0-86573-759-2

This book provides useful instructions but
we cannot anticipate all of your working
conditions or the characteristics of your
materials and tools. For safety, you should
use caution, care and good judgement
when following the procedures described in
this book. Consider your own skill level and
the instructions and safety precautions
associated with the various tools and
materials shown.

Creative Publishing international, WSP
Marketing International Ltd., Canadian Tire
Corporation, Limited, or the Canadian Tire
Associate Dealers do not assume any
responsibility for damage to property
or injury to persons as a result of the use
of the information contained in this book.

Before commencing any project, consult
your local Building Department for information on building permits, codes and other
laws, as they may apply to your project.

INTRODUCTION

The heart of all your home repair, remodelling or woodworking projects is your workshop. The tools you choose to keep in your workshop and how well this space is organized can determine how your work turns out – and how much you'll enjoy doing it. *The Essential Workshop* is full of practical information to help you accomplish these goals without spending a fortune. It's also full of useful tips on maintaining tools, helpful hints for using materials you have on hand, and even tricks for turning scrap materials into useful workshop items.

The Essential Workshop is divided into sections which cover different workshop topics: from choosing the Mastercraft tools that are right for you, to designing a layout that makes the best use of your available space – even how to set up the shop area with enough power and light. You'll also learn how to minimize noise levels and transport materials to the shop from the building centre. You'll even find a number of useful projects you can make that will help you create an efficient, functional workshop. Detailed, step-by-step instructions and full-colour photographs show you the tools needed and the building techniques required.

Have fun creating and using a practical workshop that meets your needs. Welcome to the world of Mastercraft Do-It-Yourself Guides!

TABLE OF CONTENTS

TOOL BASICS

To have a useful workshop, you will need a quality tool collection. Luckily, a well-rounded tool collection does not require a large initial investment. You can build a collection step-by-step by buying tools as they are needed.

Quality tools, like Mastercraft, carry full parts and labour warranties. Good hand tools carry a lifetime warranty.

The starter tool set includes mainly hand tools, with only a few power tools. In the right hands, these tools are suitable for many workshop projects, and they won't take up much space. Remember that not long ago, builders and hobbyists didn't have the luxury of power tools. Yet they produced beautiful, high-quality work with simple hand tools.

The intermediate tool set will allow you to work more quickly and tackle larger and more complicated projects.

The advanced tool set, with items like a table saw, will allow you to build almost anything in your workshop, provided you have adequate space for these tools.

Starter tool set *should include a generous collection of hand tools, plus a ³⁄₈" power drill, cordless screwdriver and a palm sander. Inspect the finish on hand tools; quality tools are made of high-carbon steel and have clean-cut metal surfaces. Tool handles should be tight and comfortable. Vise (A), corded drill (B), glue gun (C), palm sander (D), caulk gun (E), putty knife (F), safety glasses (G), cordless drill (H), carpenter's level (I), wood plane (J), tape measure (K), utility knife (L), chalk line (M), wire stripper/cutter (N), multimeter/circuit tester (O), drill bits, including screwdriver bits (P), ratchet set (Q), C-clamp (R), pry bar (S), nail puller (T), small Robo-Grip® pliers (U), large Robo-Grip pliers (V), needlenose pliers (W), hex key wrenches (X), groove joint pliers (Y), wrench set (Z), carpenter's square (AA), pipe wrench (BB), hammer (CC), combination square (DD), mitre box (EE), wallboard saw (FF), nail sets (GG), mitre box saw (HH), handsaw (II), screwdrivers (JJ), wood chisels (KK). A stationary or portable workbench (not pictured) is also an important workshop element.*

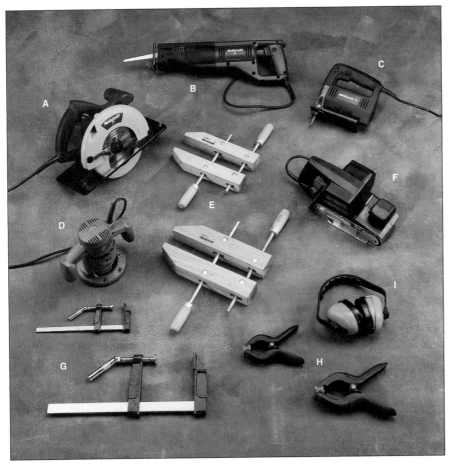

Intermediate tool collection contains everything in the starter set plus additional power tools and special purpose hand tools. Your workshop should allow you to store your power tools safely away from your work area. Circular saw (A), reciprocating saw (B), jigsaw (C), router (D), wood clamps (E), belt sander (F), bar clamps (G), spring clamps (H), ear protection (I).

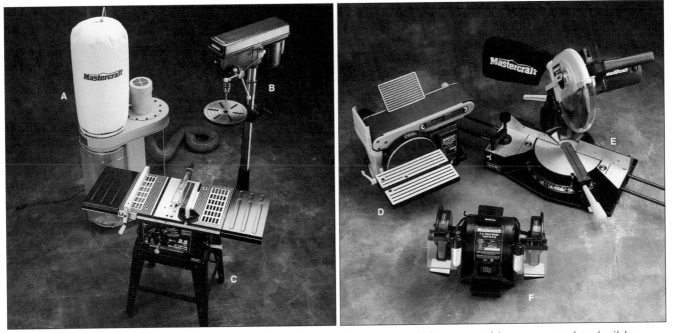

Advanced tool set includes all the tools from the previous sets and has everything you need to build a new house or construct a top-quality dollhouse. These tools require much more space in your workshop. Your workshop must also have electrical circuits that can withstand the draw of these tools. Dust collection system (A), drill press (B), table saw (C), belt/disc sander (D), power mitre saw (E), bench grinder (F). Other tools, like a bandsaw, lathe, scroll saw, jointer or wood planer, can be added depending on the types of projects you want to build.

Measuring & Layout Tools

One of the most important steps in any project is measuring distances and angles accurately.

The first place to start is with a steel tape measure with a ¾"-wide blade. Choose a tape that has the blade marked every 16" for easy layout of stud or joist locations, and make sure the lock is easy to activate.

A combination square is a compact tool used to measure and mark 45° and 90° angles. Use a framing square to lay out 90° angles. Choose a T-bevel with a locking handle to measure and transfer any angle.

To check if surfaces are plumb and level, buy a quality 2' or 4' carpenter's level made of metal or wood. You may find both sizes helpful, depending on the projects you build. You will also need a string chalk line to lay out long, straight lines.

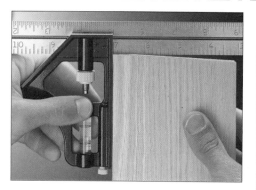

Combination square *is many tools in one. The adjustable handle has two straight surfaces for marking 90° and 45° angles. The square also has a built-in level. Some squares include a pointed metal scribe to mark wood for cutting.*

Carpenter's level *has a plumb vial for checking vertical surfaces and a level vial for checking horizontal surfaces. Level shows correct position when bubble is exactly between the line markings.*

Handsaws

For smaller jobs or occasional use, handsaws can be superior to power saws.

The crosscut saw is a standard cutting tool designed to cut across the wood grain. A crosscut saw may also be used for the occasional "rip" cuts parallel to the wood grain. A crosscut saw with 10 teeth per inch is a good choice for general-purpose cutting.

A backsaw, used with a mitre box, makes straight, very accurate cuts. The reinforced spine keeps the backsaw blade from flexing. The mitre box locks at any angle for cutting precise mitres and bevels.

A coping saw makes curved cuts on materials like wood moulding. The coping saw has a very narrow, flexible blade held taut by a C-shaped spring frame. To adjust blade position

Backsaw with mitre box *makes precise cuts at whatever angle you want. Make certain that the mitre box is securely fastened to the worksurface.*

for scroll cuts, rotate the spigots holding the blade.

Hacksaws are designed to cut metal. Like a coping saw, a hacksaw has a fine, flexible blade that can be replaced when it becomes dull.

It is important to keep handsaw cuts square to the face and sides of the workpiece. Make the job easier by building a squaring guide from scrap hardwood or plywood. Use a combination square to check each piece for squareness before assembling.

TIPS:

Hold the handsaw at a 90° angle to make fast cuts where a good edge is not important. This technique leaves a rough-edged finish.

❖❖❖❖❖❖❖❖❖❖❖❖

Hold the handsaw at a 45° angle for most cutting jobs. This will produce a fairly smooth cut and still allow you to cut quickly.

❖❖❖❖❖❖❖❖❖❖❖❖

Hold the handsaw at a 20° angle to make very smooth cuts. Sawing at this angle requires extra cutting time.

Nails & Hammers

Nail lengths are identified by numbers from 4 to 60 followed by the letter "d". Some specialty nails are identified by either length or gauge. Many nail manufacturers will explain on the box what kind of applications their nails are best designed for.

For general framing work, use either box or common nails. Box nails are smaller in diameter, which makes them less likely to split wood. Common nails are preferable for heavy framing work. Most common and box nails have a cement or vinyl coating that improves their holding power. For outdoor projects, use nails coated with zinc, which will help resist rust.

Finish and casing nails have small heads and are driven just

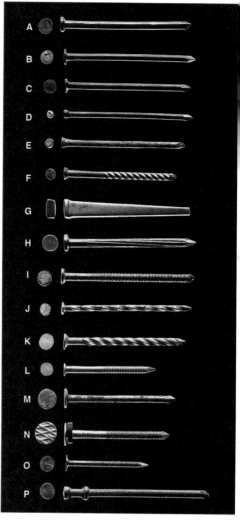

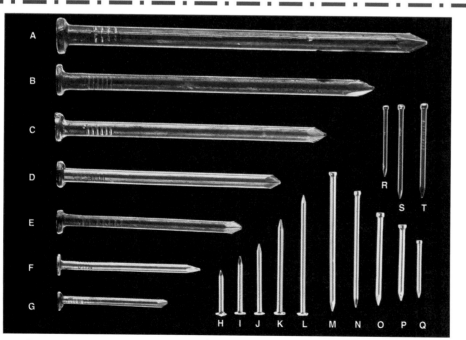

Nail sizes: 20d (A), 16d (B), 10d (C), 8d (D), 6d (E), 5d (F), 4d (G); wire nail lengths 1/2" (H), 3/4" (I), 1" (J), 1 1/4" (K), 1 1/2" (L); brad nail lengths 1 1/2" (M), 1 1/4" (N), 1" (O), 3/4" (P), 1/2" (Q); wire nail lengths 19 (R), 18 (S), 17 (T).

Types of nails: common nail for heavy-duty framing (A), box nail for light work or thinner materials (B), cement-coated sinker nail for outside sheathing (C), finish nail for fastening wood trim (D), galvanized casing nail for outside trim (E), spiral flooring nail for subflooring (F), cement cut flooring nail for fastening boards to concrete (G), masonry nail for brick and concrete (H), galvanized ring-shanked siding nail (I), galvanized spiral siding nail (J), aluminum cedar siding nail (K), aluminum cedar fence nail (L), galvanized roofing nail (M), self-sealing galvanized roofing nail for metal roofs (N), drywall nail (O), duplex nail for temporary construction (P).

below the worksurface with a nail set, for projects like nailing wood trim. Casing nails have slightly larger heads than finish nails for better holding power. Other specialty nails are identified by their intended function. These include wallboard nails, siding nails, masonry nails, flooring nails and roofing nails.

No matter what style of hammer you use, choose one with a high-carbon, smoothly finished steel head and a quality handle made of hickory, fibreglass or solid steel. Avoid bargain hammers that have rougher, painted finishes with visible cast marks.

The most frequently used hammer for carpentry is the **16-ounce curved claw hammer**. It is designed only for driving, setting or pulling nails. For all other striking jobs, use a specialty hammer.

A **ball peen hammer** is needed to pound hardened metal tools, like masonry chisels or pry bars, because it has a heat-treated steel head that resists chipping.

A **tack hammer**, which has a magnetic head, drives nails and tacks that are too small to hold.

A **rubber-head mallet** drives wood chisels or taps wood joints into place without damaging the wood.

For all metal-headed hammers, clean the hammer face periodically. Wood resins and nail coatings can build up on the face, causing the hammer to slip and mar the worksurface or bend the nail.

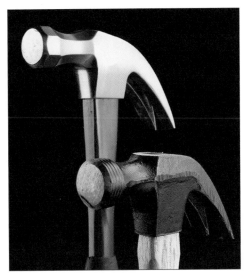

Claw hammers should be used only for driving or pulling nails. A quality hammer, left, has a smooth, high-carbon steel head. A bargain tool, right, has visible cast marks and a rougher painted finish.

Turn your ordinary claw hammer into a mini nail-puller by filing a small notch into one claw, using a triangular needle file. The small notch will make it much easier to remove finish nails and brads.

Screws & Screwdrivers

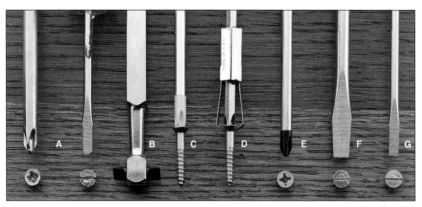

Choose the proper screwdriver for the job. *Screwdrivers should fit the screw slot tightly. Don't use a head that is too small, too large or worn. All three will strip the screw. Worn screwdrivers (A) can slip and damage screwheads and workpieces. Offset screwdriver (B) drives screws in cramped spaces. Magnetic screwdriver (C) is useful when driving small screws that are difficult to hold by hand. Screw holder (D) is useful in cramped areas where screw cannot be held by hand. Black oxide tip (E) on phillips screwdriver improves control of tool. Wide slot screwdriver (F) is correct for this screw head. Narrow slot screwdriver (G) is too small for this screw head.*

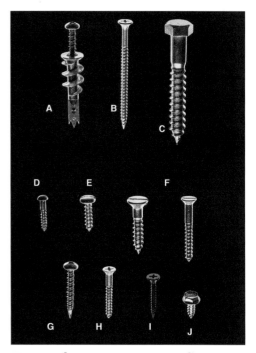

Types of screws vary according to use. *Use a screw only for its intended purpose. In other words, do not attempt to join wood with a sheetmetal screw. When you have a choice, use phillips-head screws instead of slotted screws. They are easier to drive without slipping, especially if you use a power screwdriver. Grip-it® twist anchor screw (A), galvanized utility screw (B), lag screw (C), round-head wood screw (D), pan-head sheetmetal screw (E), flat-head slotted wood screws (F), hi-low screw (G), flat-head phillips wood screw (H), wallboard screw (I), hex-head sheetmetal screw (J).*

A good workshop should have an assortment of hand screwdrivers. A quick way to botch a job is to use the wrong size or type of screwdriver. Quality screwdrivers have hardened-steel blades and wide handles that provide a good grip.

The reason you will need so many screwdrivers is because of the huge variety of screws available. Screws are categorized according to length, slot size, head shape and gauge. The thickness of the screw body is indicated by the gauge number, from 0 to 24. The larger the gauge number, the larger the screw. Large screws provide additional holding power, while small screws are less likely to split a workpiece.

When joining two lengths of wood, choose a screw length so that the entire threaded portion will extend into the base piece. Where appearance is important, use countersink or counterbore bits to drill a recessed hole that will hide the screw head. A countersink bit lets you drive a flat-head screw flush with the wood surface, while a counterbore bit lets you recess the screw head to hide the location afterward with a wood plug.

TIP:
Square head (or Robertson) screws provide better contact between the screwdriver tip and the screw than most screw types, and are therefore much harder to strip.

Clamps & Vises

Once you have a complete set of clamps and vises in your workshop, you will wonder how you ever made do without them. If you plan on doing any gluing, sanding, repairing or fine woodworking, then you will need a good assortment of clamps and vises in your workshop. Of course, you will need to use these tools correctly to get good results.

Clamps with metal jaws can damage a workpiece, so attach scrap wood blocks between the clamp jaws and the workpiece.

For wide clamping jobs, use pipe clamps or bar clamps. The jaws of these clamps are connected by ordinary steel pipe. Therefore, the distance between the jaws is limited only by the length of the pipe.

A strap clamp, which tightens a length of strap, is invaluable for gluing furniture and wood projects.

Handscrews are wooden clamps with two adjusting screws. These clamps, with their wide wood jaws, are unlikely to damage the surface of your project. Handscrews are used to hold materials together while gluing, and the screws adjust to fit angled workpieces.

Three-way clamps have three thumbscrews and are used to hold edge mouldings to the side of shelves, tabletops or other flat surfaces. As with any metal-jawed clamp, use scraps of wood to protect the surface of workpieces.

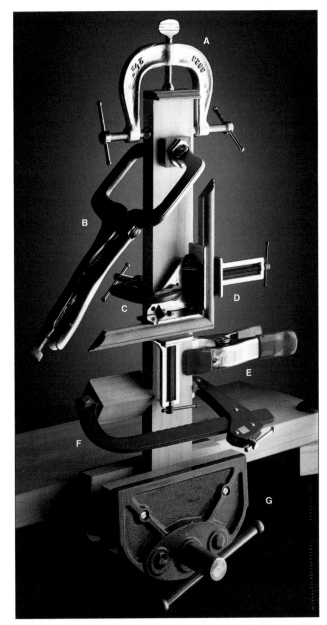

Clamp styles: *Three-way clamp (A) holds moulding and other small items to workpiece. Locking pliers (B) provide fast clamping. C-clamps (C) are the workhorses of the workshop. Corner clamps (D) are useful in framing. Spring clamps (E) are another way to clamp items quickly. Quick clamp (F) works like a C-clamp, but is faster to use. The carpenter's vise (G) holds projects securely on a workbench.*

Pliers, Sockets & Wrenches

How often you use pliers, wrenches and sockets depends on what kind of projects you tackle. The woodworker may use them only infrequently. But electricians, plumbers or mechanics could not do their jobs without these tools.

If you're buying new tools, look for pliers, wrenches and socket sets that come with a lifetime warranty, such as Mastercraft.

Pliers are designed to either hold things, snip them or both. Adjustable groove joint (A) allows you to grasp small and large items; lineman's style (B), with a built-in wire cutter, is good for electrical work; needlenose style (C) is useful for grasping tiny items or recessed wires, and diagonal style (D) is used for cutting wire. Robo-Grip pliers (E), adjust automatically to any size object and can be used with only one hand.

Whatever style, pliers are not meant to be substitutes for wrenches. Do not attempt to tighten bolts or nuts with pliers. Doing so will damage the heads of the bolts and nuts.

Quality wrenches (F), made of alloys such as chrome vanadium steel, will save you lots of grief and prevent rounding of nut heads. Make certain you have wrenches that are long enough to provide enough torque for the job. And most important, make certain you use the right size wrench for the job. A workshop should have both metric and SAE wrenches. If you're working on metric-sized bolts, use metric wrenches. The same goes with SAE. A ratcheting box wrench (G) is a wrench with ratcheting action for fast work in a tight space inaccessible to a ratchet/socket.

A pipe wrench (H) is needed for many plumbing repairs. When using this heavy wrench, protect chrome pipes by wrapping them with a scrap piece of cloth.

A socket and ratchet (I) will remove a nut faster than a wrench and is often necessary to reach into cramped spaces. The same rules apply to sockets that apply to wrenches: Use metric sockets on metric-sized bolts and nuts and SAE sockets on SAE bolts and nuts.

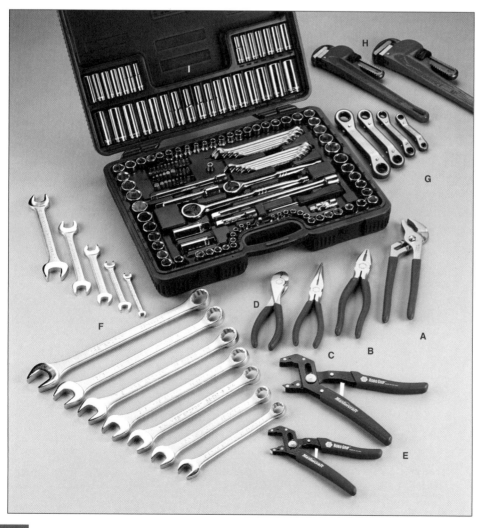

Adhesives

ADHESIVE TYPE	CHARACTERISTICS	USES
White Glue	**Strength:** Moderate; rigid bond **Drying time:** Several hours **Resistance to heat:** Poor **Resistance to moisture:** Poor **Hazards:** None **Clean-up/Solvent:** Soap and water	**Porous surfaces:** Wood, paper, cloth
Yellow Carpenter's Glue	**Strength:** Moderate to good **Drying time:** Several hours **Resistance to heat:** Moderate **Resistance to moisture:** Moderate **Hazards:** None **Clean-up/Solvent:** Soap and water	**Porous surfaces:** Interior wood, paper, cloth
Two-part Epoxy	**Strength:** Excellent **Drying time:** Varies **Resistance to heat:** Excellent **Resistance to moisture:** Excellent **Hazards:** Fumes are toxic and flammable **Clean-up/Solvent:** Acetone will dissolve some types	**Smooth & porous surfaces:** Wood, metal, masonry, glass, fibreglass
Hot Glue	**Strength:** Depends on type **Drying time:** Less than 60 seconds **Resistance to heat:** Fair **Resistance to moisture:** Good **Hazards:** Can cause burns **Clean-up/Solvent:** Heat will loosen bonds	**Smooth & porous surfaces:** Wood, plastics, glass
Cyanoacrylate Glue	**Strength:** Excellent, but little flexibility **Drying time:** A few seconds **Resistance to heat:** Excellent **Resistance to moisture:** Excellent **Hazards:** Can bond to skin instantly; toxic, flammable **Clean-up/Solvent:** Soap and water (while wet)	**Smooth surfaces:** Glass, ceramics, plastics, metal
Latex Acrylic Panel Adhesive	**Strength:** Good to excellent **Drying time:** 24 hours **Resistance to heat:** Good **Resistance to moisture:** Excellent **Hazards:** May irritate skin and eyes **Clean-up/Solvent:** Soap and water (while wet)	**Porous surfaces:** Framing lumber, plywood and panelling, wallboard, foam panels, masonry
Water-base Contact Cement	**Strength:** Good **Drying time:** Bonds instantly; dry in 30 minutes **Resistance to heat:** Excellent **Resistance to moisture:** Good **Hazards:** May irritate skin and eyes **Clean-up/Solvent:** Soap and water (while wet)	**Porous surfaces:** Plastic laminates, plywood, flooring, cloth
Silicone Sealant	**Strength:** Fair **Drying time:** 24 hours **Resistance to heat:** Good **Resistance to moisture:** Excellent **Hazards:** May irritate skin and eyes **Clean-up/Solvent:** Acetone	**Smooth & porous surfaces:** Wood, porcelain, fibreglass, plastics, glass

The cap iron should be set 1/16" back from the tip of the plane's blade.

❖❖❖❖❖❖❖❖❖❖❖❖

If the plane's cutter leaves a score mark on the wood, check to be sure the lateral adjustment is correct.

Planes & Chisels

Many woodworking or home repair projects require that you have these tools. With them, you will be able to reduce the size of a sticky door, produce a hinge or lock mortise, smooth a rough edge and more.

As with any cutting tool, it's important to keep the cutting blades sharp. Also, it's better to make several shallow cuts instead of one deep cut. Forcing a tool to make deep cuts may ruin both the tool and the workpiece.

A properly set plane will remove wood shavings that are paper thin. Cut too thick and you may gouge the wood.

Mortise Chiselling

To cut a mortise, first trace the outline of the mortise on the wood. Cut along the trace-line with the chisel to the required depth. Then, make a series of parallel cuts across the mortise, driving the chisel with light mallet blows to butt end of chisel. When that is done, lever out the waste chips by holding the chisel at a low angle with bevel side to wood and tapping gently with the mallet.

To operate a plane smoothly, grip toe knob and handle firmly, and plane with long, even strokes. To prevent "dipping" (overplaning at the beginnings and ends of boards), press down on the toe of the plane at the beginning of the stroke and bear down on the heel at the end of a stroke.

Prying Tools

It is easy to skimp on buying good prying tools. Too often, people think they can accomplish a prying job with a simple carpenter's hammer or an old screwdriver. They're making a big mistake. Using a tool incorrectly – such as using a hammer as a pry bar – is dangerous. Tools can break if used improperly. They will also damage your workpiece.

Quality prying tools, on the other hand, are safer to use and are less likely to mar your work. Good prying tools are made of high-carbon steel.

They are available in many sizes, but always choose one that is forged from a single piece. Tools made from welded parts are not as strong as those that are forged.

Wear safety glasses when working with prying tools. The tremendous pressure generated by even a small bar can catapult debris with great force.

Always protect the finished surface behind where you are prying by inserting a piece of scrap wood between the tool and worksurface.

TIP:

A prying tool called a cat's paw has a sharpened claw, useful for removing hard-to-get nails. To extract nails, drive the claw into the wood under the nail head with a hammer.

Prying tools include *wrecking bars for heavy demolition work (A), cat's paws, which are a type of nail puller, for removing nails (B) and a brad puller (C). Pry bars (D) are made of flattened steel and come in a variety of sizes for light and heavy use.*

Drills

The hand-held power drill is often the first electric tool purchased by the novice do-it-yourselfer, and for good reason. Compared to an old-fashioned hand drill, a power drill will save lots of time and effort – and it will help you do better work.

Power drills are commonly available in ¼", ⅜" and ½" sizes. The fraction refers to the largest bit shank diameter that fits the drill chuck. A ⅜" drill is often a good choice because it accepts a wide range of bits and accessories. A variable-speed reversing drill will adapt to many uses, such as drilling masonry, or driving and removing wallboard screws.

Cordless drills, which come with a rechargeable battery-pack in voltages from 7.2 to 12 offer freedom from extension cords. If you're going to be operating the drill for an extended period, purchase another battery so one can be charging while the other is running the drill.

When choosing a drill, look for quality features like an extra-long power cord with reinforced cord protector and a sealed switch that prevents dirt from entering the trigger. Also look for a drill that runs both forward and in reverse and that has a trigger lock to set a constant speed. A drill that uses top-quality materials may actually be smaller and lighter than a cheaper drill.

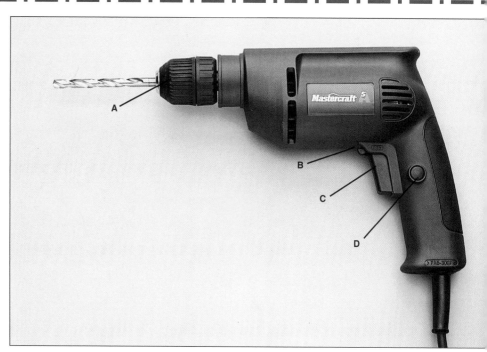

Power drill features to look for include ⅜" chuck size, variable motor speed, reversing feature, trigger lock to set a constant speed, a tough lightweight nylon housing and a heavy power cord with reinforced protector. Keyless chuck (A), reversing switch (B), variable-speed trigger (C), trigger lock (D).

Drill Bits

You'll choose the type of drill bit depending upon what task is at hand. Protect bits from rust by cleaning them with linseed oil before storing them.

A **twist bit** can be used in both metal or wood. They range from tiny wire gauge to more than ½" wide. Most twist bits are made from high-speed or carbon steel, although if you're going to be drilling into steel or other hard metals, choose a titanium or cobalt bit. Some twist bits have a self-piloting point for accurate drilling. With any twist bit, remember to drill through wood at high speeds and metal at low drill speeds.

Spade bits have a long point and flat edge cutters and are useful for cutting through wood quickly and accurately. Begin drilling at a slow speed, then increase the tempo as the bit gradually penetrates the wood.

Hole saws cut large, smooth holes through wood, like those used to mount door locksets. Make sure that the twist bit that guides the hole saw is securely mounted in the saw. When using a hole saw to cut through a workpiece, like a door with finished surfaces on both sides, care must be taken to prevent splintering on the back side of the cut. First cut from one side just far enough for the head of the twist bit to break through on the back side. Pull out the hole saw and use this hole to guide the hole saw in completing the cut from the back side.

Some of the bits you'll want in your tool chest: Twist bit (A) can be used in wood or metal. Self-piloting bit (B) requires no centre punch. Carbide-tipped masonry bit (C) can drill in concrete, cinder block or brick. (Use low drill speed and lubricate drill hole with water to prevent overheating.) Glass & tile bit (D) drills holes in smooth, brittle surfaces. Spade bit (E) is used to drill wood. Adjustable counterbore bit (F) drills screw pilot, countersink and counterbore holes with one action. Plug cutter (G) cuts circular wood plugs used to fill counterbore holes. Hole saw (H) cuts larger smooth-sided holes through wood.

Circular Saws

Anytime you have a sizable amount of cutting to do, you'll appreciate a power circular saw. The circular saw allows you to make straight cuts in wood very quickly. Special-purpose blades also make it possible to cut metal, plaster or even concrete with the saw.

When you select a saw, make certain it has a blade size of at least 7¼". A smaller saw may not cut through 2" lumber, especially if the blade is set at a bevel position. A saw should have a motor rated for at least 13 amps.

Remember that the blade of the circular saw cuts as it rotates upward. Therefore, the top face of the workpiece may splinter. To protect finished sides, mark your measurements on the back side of the piece and cut with the finished side facing down.

Remember, too, that the circular saw is probably one of the most dangerous tools in your workshop. Take extra care when working with it. Make certain your work site is free of clutter and that your workpiece is stable. Keep your saw from binding or kicking by keeping cuts straight and by inserting a shim into the kerf (space created by the cutting path of the blade).

The circular saw is also one of the noisiest tools in a workshop. Wear ear protection at all times. Eye protection should also be worn. And, of course, keep children far away.

Ripping narrow boards like 2x4s can be dangerous and difficult. When making this kind of rip cut, support the foot of the circular saw with another board that is the same thickness as the workpiece. To keep the boards from sliding as you cut, tack thin strips of wood across the bottom of the boards to hold them in place. Make sure tacks are away from the cutting path of the saw.

To keep your saw from binding, drive a wood shim into the kerf after the cut is started. Keep the kerf open during long cuts by stopping the saw and moving the shim closer to the blade.

Use a straightedge guide *for long cuts. Clamp the straightedge on the workpiece. Keep the base-plate tight against the edge guide and move the saw smoothly.*

TIPS:

For safety, set the blade so that it projects no more than the length of one saw tooth through the bottom of the workpiece. Tighten all knobs firmly.

❖❖❖❖❖❖❖❖❖❖❖❖❖

Because circular saws draw plenty of electrical current, use an extension cord that can handle the draw. Use an extension cord that is rated for at least 1440 watts and 12 amps. The wire gauge should be at least #14. Do not use an extension cord longer than 50'. The voltage drop that occurs when longer cords are used will keep the saw from operating well and may damage the motor.

Circular saw blades include *panel blade (A) with small teeth (which will not chip thin veneer layers in plywood and panelling); combination blade (B) used for fine woodworking; carbon-tipped general purpose blade (C); abrasive blades used to cut masonry (D) or metal (E).*

Jigsaws

For cutting curves or corners, the power jigsaw is invaluable. With one, you'll be able to produce delicate scroll cuts and still have enough power to slice through metal pipe.

The cutting capacity of a jigsaw depends on its motor and the length of its blade stroke. Choose a saw rated to cut at least 2"-thick softwood and 3/4"-thick hardwood stock. Also select a variable-speed jigsaw, because different blade styles may require different cutting speeds. In general, use faster blade speeds when cutting with coarse-tooth blades and slower speeds with fine-tooth blades.

A quality jigsaw will have a heavy-gauge steel baseplate to reduce the vibration inherent in the saw's up-and-down blade action. To further minimize vibration, hold the saw tightly against the workpiece and move the saw slowly so the blade does not bend.

Just as with a circular saw, the jigsaw blade cuts on the upward stroke. Because of this, the top side of the workpiece may splinter. If the wood has a good side to protect, place this side facing down.

Jigsaw Blades

Jigsaw blades come in different designs for cutting different materials.

With fine-tooth blades that have 14 or more teeth per inch, set saw at low blade speed. Coarse blades require a faster blade speed.

Jigsaws will cut wood, metal or plastic. *To cut metal/plastic, use a fine-tooth metal cutting blade and select a slow blade speed. Support sheet metal with thin plywood in order to reduce vibration. Use emery paper or a file to smooth burred edges left by the jigsaw blade.*

Table Saws

The first stationary power tool many people purchase for their home workshop is the table saw. No hand-held saw can come close to matching its straight, clean cuts. To keep your table saw cutting safely and accurately, follow these tips:

Always use the blade guard. Most table saw accidents occur when blade guards are not used. (Although the photo on this page shows the table saw with the blade guard removed, this is done for photographic clarity only.) Always keep the blade guard in place during sawing.

Use saw blades designed for the material you are cutting. A blade designed for cutting framing lumber usually is not suitable for fine woodworking.

Clean away wood pitch, resin and glue from table saw blades with an old toothbrush and lacquer thinner.

Use a pushstick to keep your fingers away from the saw blade. This safety accessory can be purchased in plastic versions or easily built out of wood in your own workshop.

Keep your table saw clean and adjusted properly. *Pay special attention to vacuuming the inside of the motor housing and anywhere sawdust can build up. The saw should then serve you well for decades.*

TIPS:

Set the height of the saw blade so it extends no more than 1/2" above the surface of the workpiece. This minimizes the amount of exposed blade. A lower blade reduces blade friction and the chipping of wood. It also reduces the chances of touching the spinning blade.

❖❖❖❖❖❖❖❖❖❖❖❖

Inaccurate cuts, binding workpieces and kickbacks can be caused by a misaligned saw blade. Check the alignment of the saw blade to the rip fence before each work session. Distances from the rip fence to the blade should be identical from the front and the rear of the blade.

Router bits spin in a clockwise direction, so the tool has a tendency to drift to the left. For best control of the tool, feed the router from left to right so that the cutting edge of the bit feeds into the tool.

❖❖❖❖❖❖❖❖❖❖❖❖

To produce large circular cuts on a board, all you need is your router, a section of chain and a screw. Drive the screw into what will become the centre-point of the circle. Attach the chain to the screw and the router. Keep the chain taut and move the router slowly around the board.

❖❖❖❖❖❖❖❖❖❖❖❖

Motor vibrations can tighten a router base thumbscrew so it is difficult to loosen. Make your own wood router wrench by cutting a strip of hardwood, then cut a narrow slot near one end, just large enough to slip over the thumbscrew.

Routers

Furniture makers and others doing fine woodworking greatly appreciate the benefits of a router, a high-speed power tool that uses changeable bits to perform a variety of cutting and shaping tasks.

A router will spin a bit at speeds up to 25,000 revolutions per minute, giving the tool an ability to make smooth cuts in even the hardest woods.

With a router, you'll be able to create dadoes (straight grooves), decorative edging, dovetail joints, rounded corners, neatly trimmed plastic laminate, large circular cuts and scrolled lettering.

Choose a router with enough muscle to do the job right: It should be rated at one horse-power or more. You'll also want other features such as a conveniently placed on-off trigger switch and a router face guide.

When using the router, the best technique is to make a series of passes, gradually extending the bit until the cut reaches the desired depth. Pushing the tool too fast will cause the motor to bog, which will in turn result in chipped and splintered wood. Moving the router too slowly can scorch the wood. It is always a good idea to practice a cut on scrap wood.

It is important that the router is not allowed to wobble during a cut. Even the slightest wobble can ruin a workpiece. Keep the router base flat by this simple technique. Clamp a piece of scrap lumber the same thickness as the workpiece to the surface of the workbench. Rest the router base on both the scrap piece and the workpiece.

Keep your router *from wobbling when cutting edge grooves by clamping scrap lumber to both sides of the workpiece, flush with the top edge. The scrap wood also provides a surface for the router face guide to run against.*

Power Mitre Saws

The power mitre saw is a versatile, portable cutting tool that is especially useful for finish carpentry, woodworking projects and plumbing pipe cutting.

When using the power mitre saw, you'll need to keep a few things in mind: It should be anchored firmly with C-clamps to a workbench. To reduce vibration and noise, it helps to place rubber pads (either from an inner tube or carpet padding) between the saw legs and the workbench surface (photo below). And as with all power saws, never tamper with the saw blade guard.

One way to make your saw easier to use is to increase the size of the metal saw bed by attaching a layer of 3/4" particleboard or plywood over the bed (photo below). The oversized wood layer protects the metal

bed and provides extra support when cutting long boards.

A technique to cut wider boards is to place a 2x4 block on the saw table. The block raises the workpiece so more of the saw blade cuts into it. A standard mitre saw with a 10" blade makes a cut 5 1/4" long with the blade set at 90° and 4" long with the blade set at 45°. With the block in place, you'll be able to perform a maximum cut of 6 1/4" at 90° and 4 1/2" at 45°.

Saw Blades

The quality of the cut produced by a power saw depends on the type of blade you use and the speed at which the blade is forced through the workpiece. In general, let the saw motor reach full speed before cutting, and lower the saw arm slowly for best results.

A power mitre saw should be securely clamped to the workbench. Notice, too, the rubber pads added under the saw's legs and the particleboard layer on the metal saw bed.

A **16-tooth carbide-tipped blade** cuts quickly, but it produces a rougher cut.

A **60-tooth carbide-tipped blade** makes a smooth cut in both hardwoods and softwoods. It is a good all-purpose blade for general shop work.

A **precision-ground cross-cut and mitre blade** makes extremely smooth and splinter-free cuts. It is an ideal blade for your fine woodworking projects.

An **abrasive friction blade** makes fast cuts on thin steel, galvanized metals and iron pipes.

Sanders

For some small projects, the best sanding tool is a hand-held sanding block. For most everything else, though, a power sander will be a real help. Of course, what type of job you're planning to tackle will determine what type of sander you'll need. For very large areas, such as hardwood floors, you'll need a high-speed floor belt sander. For smaller jobs requiring rough, fast removal of material, a portable belt sander is preferable. Orbital sanders, often called finishing sanders, are good for removing light to medium amounts of material.

Sanders also come in various sizes. "Quarter sheet" sanders are compact and easy to handle. "One-third sheet" sanders are better for working on larger areas. Remember that high-speed sanders work well for removing lots of material quickly and slower-speed sanders can create a fine, smooth texture. Sand in steps, from coarser to finer grits.

Sandpaper

60-grit coarse: Used to remove lots of material or grind down badly scratched surfaces. Often used as initial paper in refinishing hardwood floors.

100-grit medium: Used for initial smoothing of wood.

150-grit fine: Puts a finish smoothness on wood surfaces. Use fine sandpaper to prepare wood surfaces for staining or to smooth wallboard joints.

220-grit extra-fine: Used to smooth stained wood before varnishing or between coats of varnish.

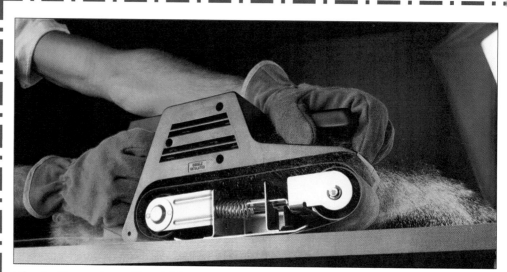

The belt sander will quickly remove material from large areas. These sanders can quickly gouge a workpiece unless they are kept moving back and forth smoothly.

Tools for Special Jobs

When you've got a big one-time project, you should probably consider renting or borrowing special tools that will make the work much easier. For example, if you are going to be framing a room addition or a storage shed, you'd be smart to rent an air-powered nailer that sinks framing nails with the squeeze of a trigger. Or if you're attaching wood framing to masonry, a gunpowder-propelled stud driver will make short work of driving masonry nails.

Tool rentals can cost just a few dollars an hour and trim hours from your schedule.

But if you regularly work on a wide range of home carpentry projects, buying the right tool could make the most sense. For the home remodeller, a reciprocating saw will slice through walls and cast-iron plumbing pipes. For anyone with many hand tools that need sharpening, a bench grinder is very useful.

An air-powered nailer or stapler is attached to an air compressor. The tool releases a burst of air to drive nails or staples into wood. If you've got a lot of work to do, this tool will save you time.

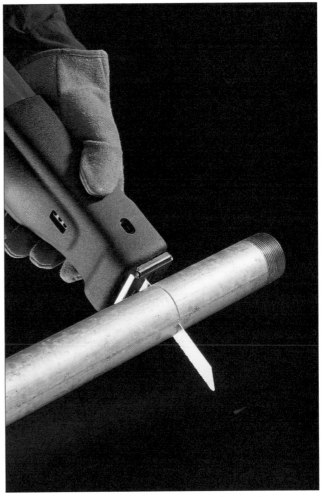

A reciprocating saw can be used for making cut-outs in walls or floors where a circular saw will not work. It is also very useful for cutting metal plumbing pipes.

Lumber & Plywood

Lumber for construction is usually milled from strong softwoods and is categorized by grade, moisture content and dimension.

GRADE: The grade is determined by characteristics such as knots, splits and the slope of the grain.

❏ Stamps of SEL, STR or select structural 1, 2 or 3 denote top grade wood that has good appearance, strength and stiffness. The numbers 1, 2 or 3 indicate knot size (1 being the best).
❏ Lumber marked CONST (or construction) or STAND (or standard) is used for general framing. It has good strength and serviceability.
❏ STUD lumber is given as a designation for lumber suitable for any stud application, including load-bearing walls.
❏ UTIL (or utility) grade lumber is bottom of the barrel, suitable for blocking and bracing.

MOISTURE CONTENT: Lumber is also categorized by how much moisture is in the wood. S-DRY (surfaced dry) designates lumber with a moisture content of 19% or less. S-DRY lumber is the least likely to warp or shrink and is a good choice for framing walls. S-GRN (surfaced green) means the lumber contains a moisture content of 19% or more.

DIMENSION: Lumber is sold according to nominal sizes throughout the industry, such as 2x4 and 2x6. The actual size of the lumber is smaller than the nominal size.

Nominal vs. Actual Lumber Dimensions

NOMINAL	ACTUAL
1x4	¾ x 3½"
1x6	¾ x 5½"
1x8	¾ x 7½"
2x4	1½ x 3½"
2x6	1½ x 5½"
2x8	1½ x 7½"

Inspect lumber for flaws. *Look along the length of each board to check for warping and twisting. Return any boards with serious flaws. Check for large or loose knots. Boards used for structural construction should be knot-free (clear), or should have only small knots that are tight and ingrown.*

To read lumber markings, *check grade stamp for grade, moisture content and species.*

Exterior Lumber

Lumber milled from redwood or cedar is naturally resistant to decay and insect attack. While expensive, it is an excellent wood for exposed applications.

The most durable part of a tree is the heartwood, so specify heartwood for wood that will be in contact with the ground.

Lumber injected under pressure with chemicals is resistant to decay, but it contains toxic chemicals, so wear a protective particle mask and gloves when working with it. Also, do not burn chemically treated lumber.

Plywood & Sheet Goods

Plywood is a versatile building material made by laminating thin layers or "plies" of wood together and forming them into panels. Plywood is available in thicknesses ranging from 3/16" to 3/4". Plywood is graded A through D, according to the quality of the wood used on its outer plies. It is also graded for interior or exterior usage. Plywood is classified by group numbers, based on the wood species used for the face and back veneers. Group 1 species are the strongest and the stiffest. Group 2 is the next strongest.

Finish plywood may have a quality wood veneer on one side and a utility-grade ply on the other side. This will be graded A-C. If it has quality veneer on both sides, it will be graded A-A.

Sheathing plywood is for structural use. It may have large knotholes that make it unsuitable for finish purposes. Sheathing plywood is rated for thickness and is graded C-D with two rough sides. It also has a waterproof bond. Plywood rated EXPOSURE 1 is for use where some moisture is present. Plywood rated EXTERIOR is used in applications that are permanently exposed to weather. Sheathing plywood

also carries a thickness rating and a roof and floor span index, which appear as two numbers separated by a diagonal slash. The first number, for roofing applications, indicates the widest allowable spacing for rafters. The second number shows the widest spacing for joists when plywood is used for a subfloor.

Strand-, particle- and waferboards are made from waste chips or inexpensive wood species and are usually used for underlayments.

Plastic laminates, such as Formica®, are durable surfaces for countertops and furniture. Particleboard is often used as the base under plastic laminates.

From top to bottom: *finish plywood (A), sheathing plywood (B), strandboard (C), particleboard with plastic laminate (D), waferboard (E), particleboard (F).*

WORKSHOP ORGANIZATION

When designing a workshop, ask yourself three questions: How much space do I have? How many tools do I have (or plan to buy)? What type of projects will I do?

The answers to all three questions should dictate how you shape your workshop. After all, if you have a small basement corner allocated for your workshop, you are not going to have space for many floor-mounted power tools. On the other hand, if you have a vast empty room, but only plan to have a small workbench and a few hand tools, there is no reason to plan a sprawling workshop.

The key is to build an efficient and safe workspace. Bigger is not necessarily better. Many exceptional craftspeople produce stunning works in small workshops. Organization and proper planning are much more important than simply raw space.

Your first task should be to sketch out ideas on graph paper. Map out potential layouts in scale. Always think several steps ahead. For example, if you someday plan on installing a table saw, make certain you'll have enough free space near the saw to feed in long pieces of lumber. If you have several hand power tools, be sure you have outlets where they are handy. If you will be producing plenty of sawdust, plan on a way to remove the dust – and do not place your workshop next to a furnace where the dust could create a fire hazard.

When you consider what tools you have – or might have someday – think how they would best be organized. For example, if

In a useful workshop, *even the smallest tools and materials should have their own place.*

you have power tools, but just a few wall outlets, do not put the power tools far from the outlets.

The same forethought goes into considering what types of projects you'll do. If you want to repair large machinery or build big furniture pieces, make certain your workshop has a large enough entryway to transport your material. Meanwhile, if you plan on painting or fine carving, where abundant natural light is very helpful, you'll want that part of your workshop next to a window.

The heart of any workshop is the workbench. Its surface should be clean and uncluttered; it should have excellent lighting and it should be close to your most commonly used tools.

Do you plan to have company in your workshop? *If more than one person will be working at one time, you may need to configure your layout differently. Do not forget that two people, each running large power tools, cause an electrical load that your shop must be wired to handle.*

In the next few pages you'll see designs for three workshops of different sizes. Read through the information for all of them to see what space, lighting and power needs match yours. You'll also see plans for a solid workbench and dozens of tips for ways to organize your workshop.

Your first step should be to sketch some ideas with a pencil and a pad of paper.

Trace the dimensions of your workshop, to scale, and then draw a variety of different layouts. Again, think of the three questions: How much space? How many tools? What kind of projects?

> **TIP:**
> You should have a ULC (United Laboratories Canada) approved smoke alarm mounted in your workshop area.

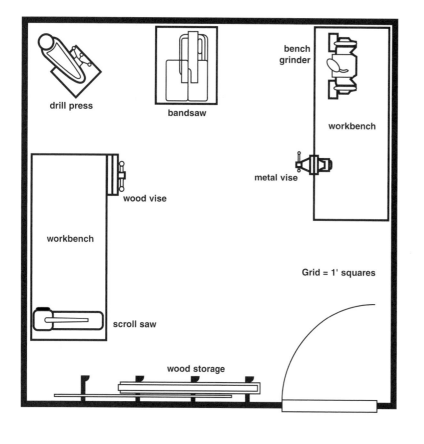

10x10'

A small workshop space is still very useful. While a table saw is not usually practical in this space, a band saw is and can accomplish many of the same tasks for smaller project pieces. A power mitre box might also be useful in this small space if it fits your needs. Moveable platforms may help you make maximum use of the workshop.

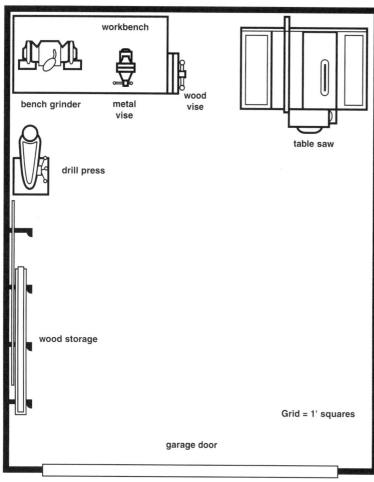

10x12'

A garage that you need to park your vehicle in is a natural place in which to use portable workshop equipment. All large tools and workbenches are mounted on moveable platforms. When you wish to work, back the vehicle out and move things into position. When you are done, clean up and move the tools back so the vehicle can be parked. In good weather you can work outside of the garage if more space is needed.

Small Space Workshop

When you have only a small space to create your shop or want just a compact workspace, do not worry. With the right organization, you can do a surprising number of projects with very limited room. Almost any house or garage has the space for a small workshop. Consider where you might have just a few extra square feet of space. The workshop might be located in the corner of a garage, a basement nook or any underused, out-of-the-way corner. For summertime projects, a great deal of work can be done under a patio roof.

For those with truly tight space, consider creating a part-time workshop that can be set up when needed. One enterprising person created a small workshop in an apartment storage locker by combining a pair of sturdy sawhorses, a sheet of plywood, a handful of clamps and a large toolbox. Another apartment dweller built a small workbench that could be slipped into place on top of the kitchen sink. For messy projects, such as sanding, this person enclosed the workpiece in a large plastic bag and created two hand openings as a way to control dust.

To have a successful small workshop, you'll need a good workbench that has plenty of storage space underneath. Shelves and upper cabinets placed over workbenches and floor standing tools efficiently provide maximum space usage for tool and material storage. You'll also need to plan your tool purchases carefully. If space is at a premium, consider hand tools instead of power tools; and if you need power tools, you may need portable tools instead of stationary tools. If space is very tight, a folding workbench can work very well. In a pinch, some sawhorses and a sheet of plywood will give you an instant workbench.

Also consider mounting workbenches or stationary tools on rolling platforms so you can move them into position when you need them and keep them out of the way when you do not. Some manufacturers provide these as an optional tool accessory you can purchase. Or you can build a sturdy platform supported by heavy-duty casters on which to mount the workbench or tool. Make sure you use casters that can be locked to keep everything immobile during use.

Before you create a workshop, consider the dimensions of lumber or other material you'll be working with. While you might not have a lot of space for tools, if you can "borrow" nearby floor space when working, you'll be able to do things like cut down long pieces of lumber or refinish a large door without bumping into walls.

TIP:

What is the most important tool in a very small workshop?

It may be a portable workbench, such as a Mastercraft folding workbench. These benches will give you a small flat surface to work upon, and the benchtop serves double-duty as a vise. Weight ratings vary, but even small folding workbenches can hold up to 400 lbs (180 kg). When not in use, these folding workbenches can be slipped into a small closet or hung on a wall.

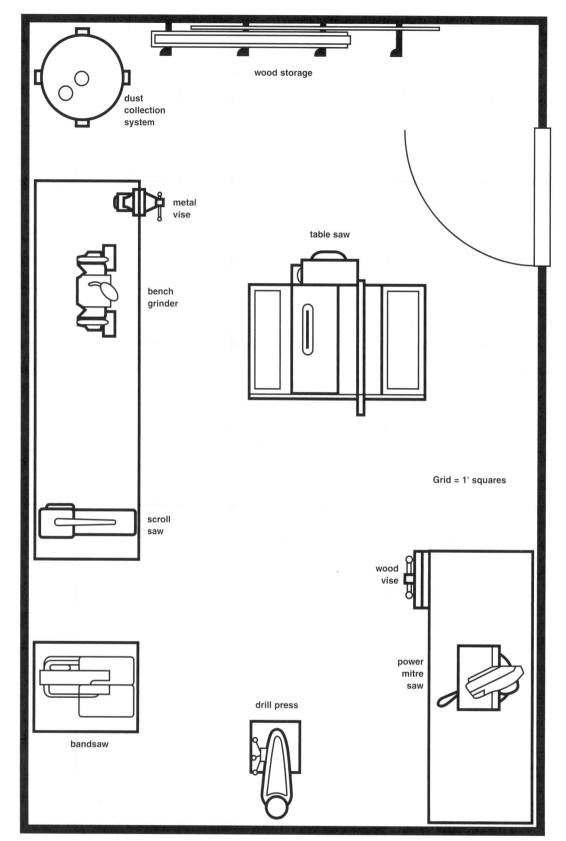

wood storage

dust collection system

metal vise

table saw

bench grinder

Grid = 1' squares

scroll saw

wood vise

power mitre saw

drill press

bandsaw

This 10x15' space *provides a fair amount of flexibility in creating a workshop. While you can use a table saw, working with large materials will be limited. Note the wood storage area is conveniently located near the door where the materials are brought in. Also the dust collection system is placed in a corner: If a duct-and-port system is used, it is out of the way; otherwise, it can be rolled into position where needed.*

Medium Space Workshop

With a medium-sized workshop (10x15'), you'll have additional room for power tools and a lot more storage space than with a small workshop nook. A basement room or a garage bay will give you the necessary space for this workshop.

Consider adding an additional workbench. Two workbench areas will give you much-appreciated space when you tackle big projects, and they'll allow you to work on two projects at the same time.

You still won't have the space to do some tasks, however. For example, to cut a full-sized 4x8' sheet of plywood lengthwise with a table saw, you'll need at least 16' of space. (If you use a garage bay, opening the garage door probably will allow for this.) But for many projects, a medium-sized workshop is ideal. There will be room to install several stationary power tools and plenty of space for hand tools.

Because you'll have the space for multiple power tools, make certain your electrical system is up to the challenge. A workshop of this size should at least have its own dedicated electrical circuit, with several well-placed receptacles. Ideally, a workshop of this size or larger should have a dedicated circuit for the lights and another for the tools. That way, if you trip a circuit breaker (or blow a fuse) because you use too many power tools, you'll still have lights in your shop. A house with an adequate electrical system will have no problem accepting the additional electrical draw of a workshop (within reason). After all, most hand power tools run on 120-volt current and draw less than 15 amps. Plus, because you shouldn't have more than one power tool on at a time, you should not find yourself overtaxing your home's safe electrical load. Of course, if you install large 240-volt stationary tools and operate electrical equipment simultaneously, such as a dust collec-tion machine and a table saw, then you may need to upgrade your electrical system to handle the load. Talk to an electrician.

The height of your worksurfaces will greatly affect how comfortable and safe your workshop is. Precise hand work, in which elbow support is needed, requires a higher worksurface than does heavy construction. A workbench for heavy work might stand 34" tall, while an area for precise work might stand 44" tall. Of course, your height will enter into the equation. If you're shorter than average, a lower surface will be appropriate and, if you're taller, a higher surface is wise. The highest worksurface for normal projects should be below elbow height, which will still permit your upper arms to hang relaxed.

Because workshops are often in basements or in the rear of garages, the original lighting is often poor. Inadequate lighting causes fatigue, poor workmanship and safety hazards.

First, consider ways to increase natural light. If you can add or increase the size of nearby windows or install a skylight, you can improve the daytime lighting of your shop and give yourself the option of having a source of fresh air. Consider moving your workbench to take best advantage of the existing natural light.

Adding fluorescent fixtures to bathe your entire shop in light is easy and inexpensive. An adequate number of fluorescent fixtures will produce a bright, shadowless room, which is ideal for most shop work. Your workbench surface should have clear, bright lighting. Stand a pencil on end on your workbench and check to be sure you do not have any shadows. For small space task lighting where some shadows are helpful – such as carving or scroll work consider shielded incandescent fixtures.

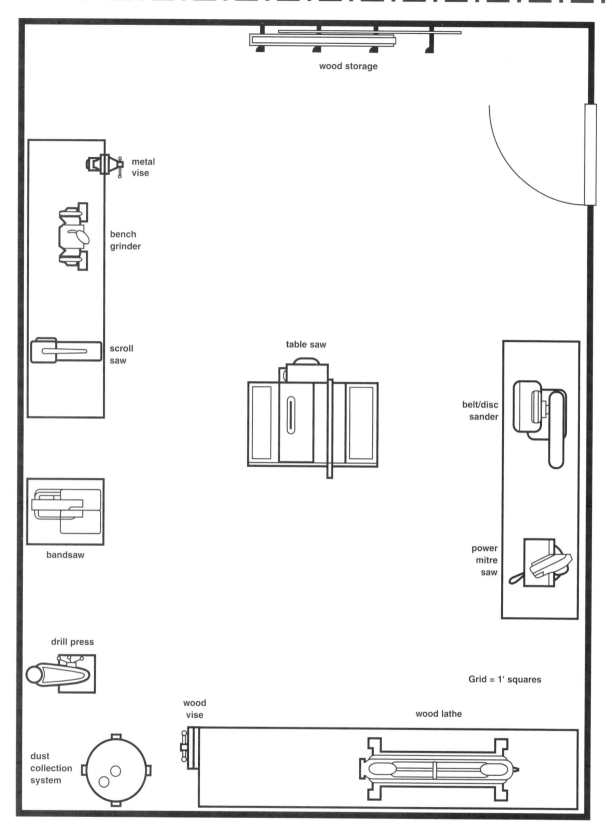

wood storage

metal
vise

bench
grinder

scroll
saw

table saw

belt/disc
sander

power
mitre
saw

bandsaw

drill press

Grid = 1' squares

wood
vise

wood lathe

dust
collection
system

A large 15x20' workshop space provides easily for almost any work you wish to do – but organization is still important so space and effort are not wasted. A centrally located table saw with plenty of clear space surrounding it allows for working with large materials, like full sheets of plywood. Wood storage is conveniently located near the door where wood is brought in, but also near the table saw where first cuts are usually made. Dust collection is close to the tools that make the most dust. Keep material clearances in mind when locating the tools that will shape them.

Large Space Workshop

With the right organization, a large 15x20' workshop will give you enough space for almost any project. A larger basement room or garage dedicated solely to your workshop will give you the necessary 300 sq. ft. of space.

A large workshop will provide ample opportunity for expanding your stationary tool collection. In a room this size, you would have no trouble installing a table saw, a power mitre box, a bandsaw, a drill press, a wood lathe and a belt/disc sander. You would still have plenty of room left over to store lumber, stepladders and ongoing projects. If you're planning to cut 4x8' sheets of plywood on a table saw, or refurbish an antique motorcycle or work with another person, you'll appreciate a large workshop.

If you do install several stationary power tools, be certain your home wiring is up to the task. Check the electrical draw of your equipment and compare it to the rated "safe" carrying capacity of your circuitry.

For more information, contact an electrician or read any of the good how-to electrical guides available for sale.

Electrical extension cords are a tool accessory best left unused if possible. A workshop floor covered with extension cords is dangerous and inefficient. The best way to reduce the need for extension cords is to have a generous amount of receptacles in a workshop. They should be placed where you use your tools. Install an outlet every 3' on your walls. Consider, too, ceiling outlets in the middle of a room. An easy way to add to the number of outlets is to install a plug-in power bar (photo below).

If you must use an extension cord, try to use only one cord at a time. Use only as long a cord as you need. When you use an extension cord, make certain it can handle the power (amps) required by the tool you are using (check tool manufacturer's specifications). An undersized extension cord can keep tools from working properly or cause short circuits.

TIP:

With a larger workshop, don't be tempted to be a pack rat. A collection of junk in your workshop will eliminate all the advantages that come with having more space. In addition, it will be much harder to locate items if you have piles of odds and ends in your workshop. And flammable materials are, of course, a fire hazard. If you're done with something, consider whether it is worth saving.

Building a Workbench

Whatever size your workshop, you'll need a sturdy workbench.

These workbench plans will give you a sturdy, stable platform. The workbench has heavy-duty legs to support big loads and a double-layer top to withstand pounding. You can easily add options to the workbench.

A hardboard surface will allow you to replace the material when it becomes damaged. A shelf below the workbench will store power tools. And you can bolt an all-purpose vise to the front or the top of this bench, or add pegboard to the bench ends for small tools.

Construction Materials

Qty.	Size	Lumber
6	2x4" x 8'	pine
1	2x6" x 5'	pine
1	4x8' x ¾"	plywood
1	4x8' x ½"	plywood
1	4x8' x ⅛"	hardboard

TIP:
Use a framing square to mark plywood and hardboard pieces, and cut with a circular saw to the proper dimensions. A power mitre box will do a great job of cutting square ends on the pine pieces.

Cutting List

KEY	PIECES	SIZE & DESCRIPTION
A	1	⅛" hardboard top, 24 x 60"
B	2	¾" plywood top, 24 x 60"
C	4	2x4 crosspieces, ends, 21"
D	4	2x4 legs, 19¾"
E	4	2x4 legs, 34½"
F	4	2x4 legs, 7¾"
G	3	2x4 braces, 54"
H	1	2x6 front (top) brace, 57"
I	1	½" plywood shelf, 14 x 57"
J	1	½" plywood backer, 26¾ x 51"
K	1	1x4 backstop, 57"

How to Build a Workbench

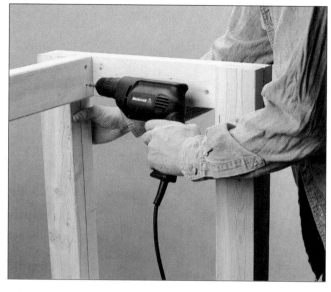

1 For each end, cut two each of pieces C, D, E and F. Assemble with 2½" wallboard screws.

2 Attach both 2x4 rear braces (G) inside back legs of assembled ends. Use 2½" wallboard screws. Attach 2x4 front lower brace (G) inside front legs of assembled ends. Secure bottom shelf (I) and workbench back (J) with 2½" wallboard screws to assembled 2x4 frame.

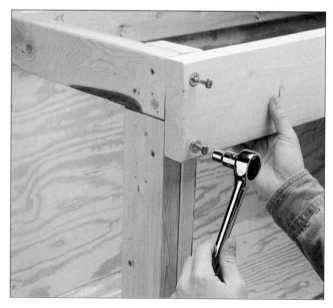

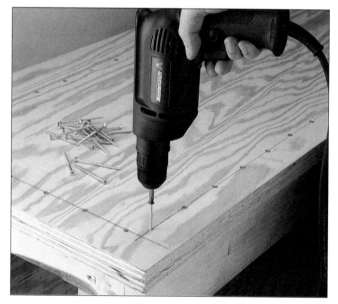

3 Drill pilot holes and join 2x6 front upper brace (H) outside front legs with 3" lag screws.

4 Centre bottom layer of ¾" plywood worksurface (B) on top of frame. Hold in place with 4d nails. Place top layer of worksurface (B) on bottom layer (B). Drive 3" wallboard screws through both layers into bench frame. Finally, nail hardboard worksurface (A) on with 4d nails. Set nails below surface with a nail punch.

Building Sawhorses

Every workshop should have a pair of sturdy sawhorses. They support material for cutting and marking and they can also form the base for sturdy temporary scaffolding. To create scaffolding, place quality 2x10s or 2x12s across two heavy-duty sawhorses. If your workshop space is limited – and you don't need sawhorses strong enough for temporary scaffolding, small break-down sawhorses are a good choice. They can be purchased at any home centre or lumberyard.

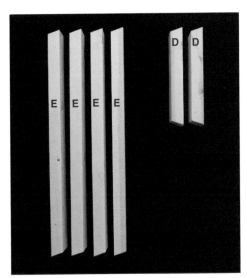

RECOMMENDED POWER TOOLS

MASTERCRAFT

DRILL

MASTERCRAFT

CIRCULAR SAW

How to Build a Sawhorse

1 Cut vertical braces (A), top rails (B) and bottom brace (C) to lengths specified in lumber Cutting List.

2 Set circular saw to 17° bevel angle to create a bevel cut. Cut ends of horizontal braces (D) with opposing angles. Cut ends of legs (E) with parallel angles.

3 Attach top rail to vertical braces (A) using 2½" wallboard screws. Attach horizontal braces (D) to vertical braces (A) using screws. Attach legs (E). To complete sawhorse, attach bottom brace (C) to horizontal braces (D).

RECOMMENDED HAND TOOLS

MASTERCRAFT

BASIC HAND TOOLS

- framing square
- screwdriver bits

NEEDED MATERIALS

- four 8' 2x4s
- 2½" wallboard screws

Cutting List

KEY	PIECES	SIZE & DESCRIPTION
A	2	2x4 vertical braces, 15½"
B	2	2x4 top rails, 48"
C	1	2x4 bottom brace, 48"
D	2	2x4 horizontal braces, 11¼"
E	4	2x4 legs, 26"

Create more space by attaching pegboard to the sides of workbenches, to the inside of cabinet doors or to the studs in unfinished utility areas. Small sections of pegboard are good for holding small tools; large sections are handy for attaching wallboard framing squares, garden tools, levels and other large items.

❖❖❖❖❖❖❖❖❖❖❖❖

Most workshops have dozens of small containers or bags holding screws, nails, bolts and other hardware. To locate items quickly, use a hot glue gun to stick a sample of the contents on the outside of each bag or box.

Organizing

It doesn't matter how large your workshop is or how many tools you have if you cannot find things when you need them. You should develop an organizational method whereby your tools are stored safely and efficiently – and where you know you can find them quickly.

One of the easiest ways to organize hand tools is to hang them on a pegboard tool hanger (below). By hanging the tools, they are in sight but out of harm's way.

Use a hot glue gun *to attach metal washers over peg holes on the back side of pegboard. Space washers to match spacing of all studs (every 16" or 24"). Use enough washers to hold the pegboard out about 1/4" from wall so tool hooks may be inserted. Then position pegboard so that holes are over studs. Drive wallboard screws.*

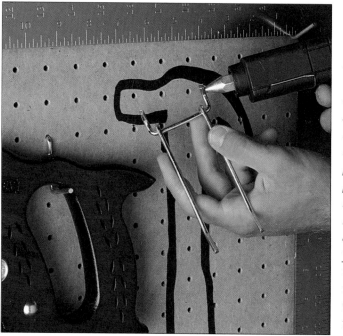

When pegboard *is mounted, trace tools with felt-tipped pens so they can be returned to the same location after use. For the final step, glue the pegboard hooks with a hot glue gun to the pegboard. This will prevent the aggravating problem of having hangers fall out when a tool is removed. If you need to reposition the hooks, heat them for a few seconds with a glue gun until the glue softens.*

Make use of storage space under an exposed stairway by building plywood shelves. Attach the shelves to the stairway stringers to store tool manuals, small cans and bottles. Attach nails and hooks to risers for storing rolls of tape, paintbrushes, putty knives and other small tools.

Attaching Pegboard to Masonry

Attach furring strips to wall with 2" masonry nails. For solid support, space the strips no more than 4' apart. For example, a 6'-long pegboard panel requires one furring strip for each end, plus a third strip to support the middle of the panel.

Position the pegboard panel against the furring strips. Drive ¾" wallboard screws through the pegboard holes and into the furring strips. Use finish washers (A) to keep the heads of the wallboard screws from sinking into the pegboard.

When attaching pegboard to masonry walls, cut 1x2" furring strips to match the height of the pegboard panel. Apply panel adhesive to one side of each strip. This will help hold the strips to the masonry walls.

Oil Can Organizer

Here is a handy way to keep extension cords and power tool cords from becoming knotted and tangled: cut off the ends of a clean plastic motor oil bottle and slip it over the coiled electrical cord. (Just make certain the inside of the bottle is completely free of oil residue.)

Overhead Help

Store long materials in the space between open ceiling joists in an unfinished utility area like a garage or basement. Attach ¾" plywood furring strips across the joists with 2½" wallboard screws or lag screws. Space the strips no more than 36" apart to provide adequate support. Make sure to avoid any electrical cables or fixtures located between the ceiling joists.

You also can attach boards across the bottom of ceiling joists to make out-of-the-way storage shelves for small cans and other shop items.

Up, Up & Away

Use large, rubber-coated lag hooks to store power tools off the floor and away from dirt and moisture. Anchor the lag hooks securely to ceiling joists or cross blocking. Make certain to locate the tools where people will not bump into them with their heads.

Don't Wear Out Your Shoes

A rolling tool cabinet containing tools and accessories you use at many work areas is a great help. This way you can keep what you need always close at hand and not waste valuable time walking for tools.

Router bits and other sharp tools *can be stored safely by lining a workbench drawer with rigid foam or foam rubber. Cut out recesses in the foam so the finely honed cutting edges do not bump against other objects.*

Keep extension cords tangle-free *by storing them in 5-gallon plastic buckets. Cut a hole in the side of the bucket near the bottom and thread the cord, prong first, through the hole. The cord will remain tangle-free when pulled from the bucket.*

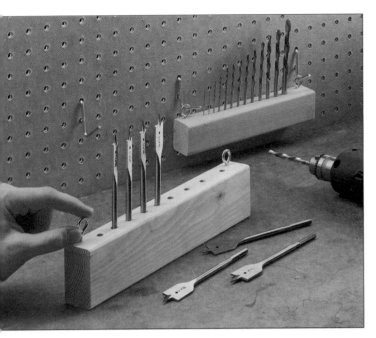

Metal drill and router bits have finely honed cutting edges that can be ruined if the bits bump against each other inside a toolbox or workbench drawer. To protect tool bits from damage, make a storage block by boring holes in a scrap piece of lumber. Attach screw eyes to the top of the block so it can be stored on pegboard hooks and taken down when a bit is needed.

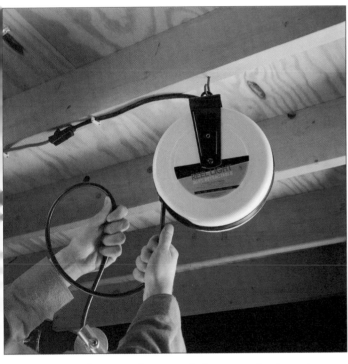

Keep extension cords out of the way by hanging retractable or reel-type extension cords from overhead hooks. They can be positioned wherever they are needed and retracted when not in use. Retractable cords are available in a variety of lengths.

Sanding Belt Storage

Sanding belts stored in a drawer or toolbox can get creased or flattened and lose their effectiveness. To avoid this, hang sanding belts from old paint-roller covers or pieces of PVC plumbing pipe that are placed over long pegboard hooks.

Make a Saw Blade Caddy

Use a plywood scrap to make a convenient caddy for storing saw blades and carrying them to a job site. Use a jigsaw to cut a carrying handle in the top of a piece of plywood 2" wider and 3" taller than the diameter of the saw blades. Drill a 3/8" hole through the plywood, and secure the blades with a 3" carriage bolt, wing nut and washer. Place cardboard between the blades to protect the teeth from damage.

Key to Safe Tool Use

Prevent children from using power tools by inserting spring-metal key rings through the small holes on the prongs of the plug. Or use small, key-operated luggage padlocks to safeguard against unauthorized tool use.

More Power to You

If you are upgrading your electrical service, have an electrician install a sub-panel near the shop to control the circuits that serve it. A nearby subpanel is convenient if a circuit breaker trips or a fuse blows. With a subpanel, you can also turn off workshop circuits and lock the subpanel cover to prevent unauthorized tool use.

Simple Clamp Storage

Organize a collection of pipe clamps, bar clamps and Quick Grips by storing them on a 2x4 attached to wall studs. Anchor the 2x4 to the studs with 3" wallboard screws or lag screws, using two screws per stud.

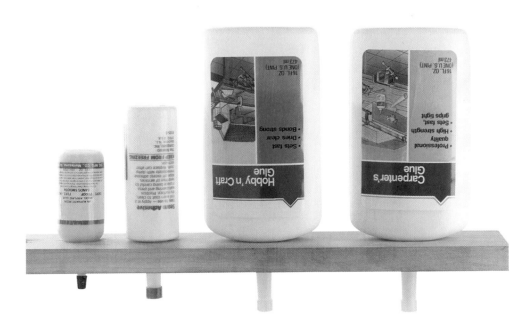

Ready-to-go Glue

Store glue bottles upside down so the glue is ready to pour whenever it is needed. Make a glue bottle holder by drilling holes in a scrap 1x4 and attaching it to a wall or a pegboard storage panel.

Getting Things Home

Transporting building material from the lumberyard or home centre to your workshop is often the first step in a project. It can be the most difficult. While framing lumber can often be tied to a vehicle roof carrier rack, sheets of plywood, panelling or wallboard should be delivered by truck. If you don't have use of a truck, many lumberyards will deliver your materials for a small charge.

Material carried atop a car must be securely attached. If the material extends past the rear bumper, tie a red flag to the load to warn other drivers.

For very heavy material, such as brick or sand, check your vehicle's weight capacity. Even a small trunk-load (9 cu. ft.) of sand, for example, can weigh well over 1,000 lbs (450 kg).

To carry full-sized sheets of plywood, panelling or wallboard by yourself, tie a single length of rope, about 18' long, in a loop. Hook the ends of the loop over the lower corners of the sheet and grip the middle of the rope in one hand. Use the other hand to balance the sheet.

TIP:

You have to carry material on your vehicle roof but you don't have roof racks? Don't worry. A handy substitute is a set of inexpensive, vinyl-coated roof brackets and nylon packing straps. Hook the brackets over the edge of the roof, then cinch the packing straps over your material, which should be centred on your roof. To prevent scratches to your roof, place a carpet scrap under the material.

When you know the cutting dimensions of sheet goods, cut the materials to size while still at the lumberyard. Some lumberyards will cut for free, or bring a saw and cut it yourself.

Workshop Soundproofing

The noise generated by some power tools, such as circular saws and routers, can reach 115 decibels. That's enough to cause permanent hearing loss in just a short time. Remember, too, that noise from very loud tools is a nuisance throughout the house – and even the neighbourhood. Soundproofing your workshop will go a long way to improving your comfort and that of your family and neighbours.

Noise levels in a workshop can be controlled by reducing the sound-causing vibrations of power tools (see example on page 25). In addition, you can soundproof walls and ceilings to prevent noise from being carried beyond the workshop.

Wall construction is rated for noise by the Sound Transmission Class (STC) system. The higher the STC rating, the less sound will transmit through it. The chart (opposite page) shows different wall constructions and rates their ability to reduce sound.

Workshop doors with hollow-core construction carry sound well. Deaden the doors by attaching acoustical tile to the inside surface. The tiled door can also be used as a bulletin board.

Air gaps in walls and ceilings can carry a substantial level of sound. To limit the amount of noise (and dust) escaping to other rooms, install door sweeps to seal the gaps underneath workshop doors and use fibreglass insulation to plug the holes near water pipes and the spaces between ceiling joists.

Soundproofing Walls & Ceilings

Sound Transmission Class (STC)

Typical utility-area stud wall, unfinished on one side. Wall stud (A), wallboard (B).

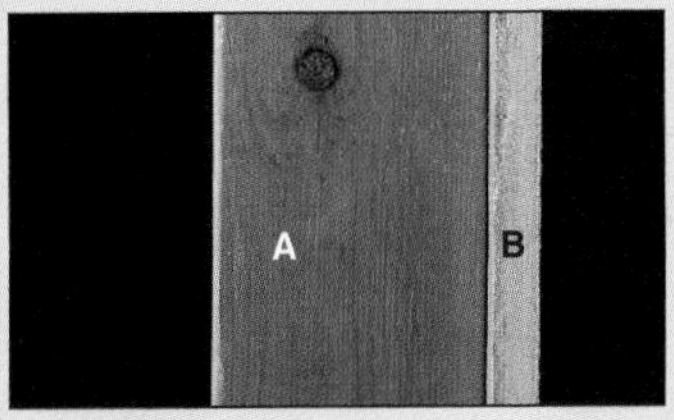

STC 28
Power tool noise is loud enough to cause permanent hearing loss with prolonged exposure.

Finish the workshop side of the wall with ½" wallboard (C).

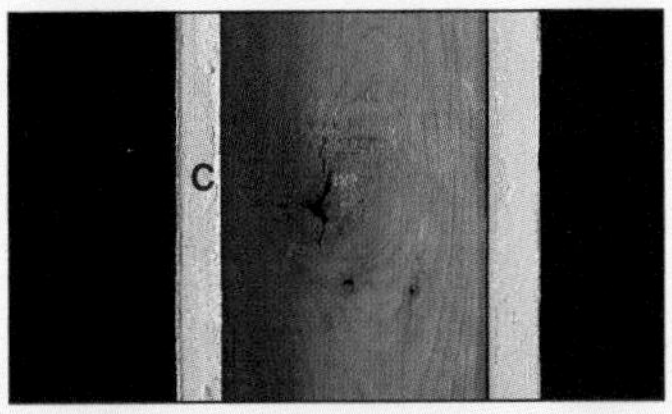

STC 34

Fill spaces beyween framing members with fibreglass insulation (D) and cover with wallboard.

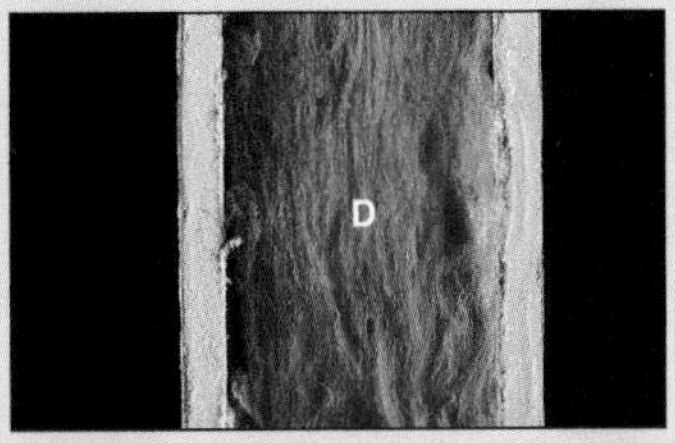

STC 39

Add an extra layer of wallboard (E) to the shop side of the insulated stud wall.

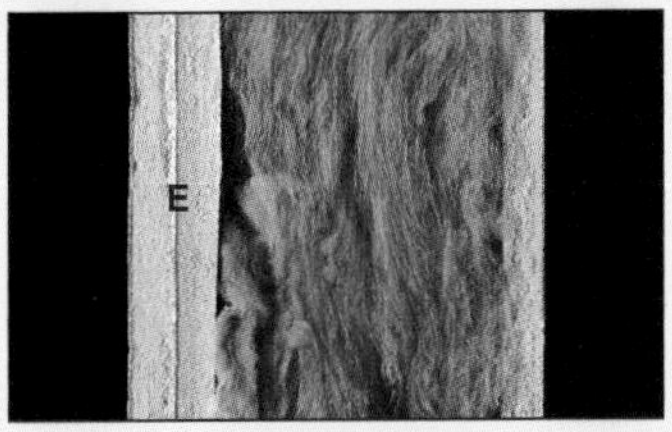

STC 42

Attach an extra layer of wallboard to wall, using resilient steel channels (F). Attach channels every 24".

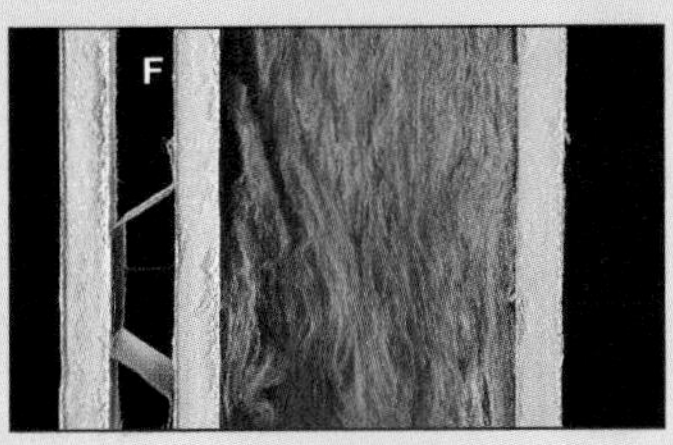

STC 44

Attach acoustical tile (G) to the insulated stud wall, using construction adhesives or staples.

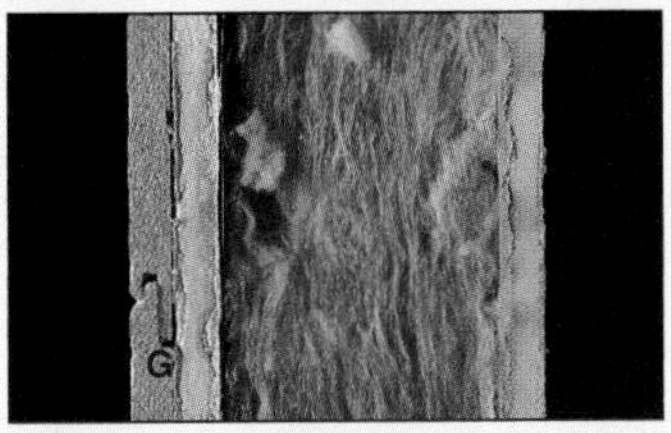

STC 46

Attach ½" fibreboard (H) and an extra layer of wallboard to walls.

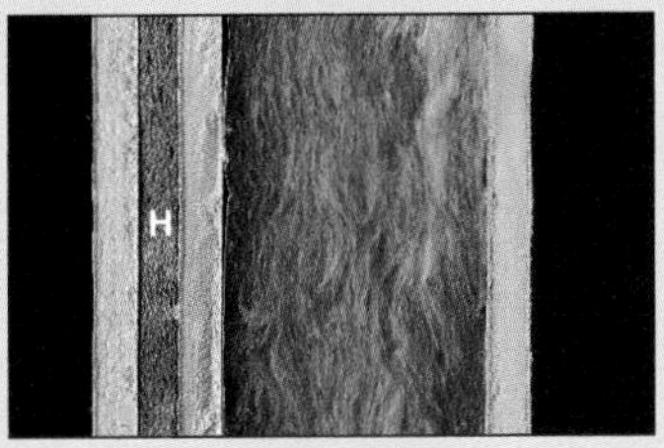

STC 50
Power tool noise is barely audible.

Store flammable materials *such as solvents and paints in a locked metal cabinet away from sources of heat and flame. Keep a fire extinguisher in the shop where you can reach it in a hurry. Your workshop should also have a smoke detector. To further reduce fire hazards, place loose sawdust and wood chips in a covered metal trash can and empty it frequently.*

It does not matter how beautiful a project is if you take unnecessary risks while making it. To create a good workshop, you need to think about ways to eliminate fire, electric shock, cuts and hazardous fumes. A well-functioning workshop also has an absence of moisture, sawdust, dirt and disorganization. The following pages contain some important guidelines that will make your shop – and your home – a safer, more pleasant place to be.

Workshop Safety & First-Aid Are Priorities

Safety is the number one priority in the workshop. Keep a well-stocked basic first-aid kit in your workshop. Equip your kit with a variety of bandages, antiseptic ointment, cotton swabs, eye drops, a first-aid handbook, a chemical cold pack, elastic bandage, first-aid tape and sterile gauze. Remember to wash any cut with soap and water and apply antiseptic ointment promptly.

Seek medical help for puncture wounds, deep cuts and other serious injuries.

If you're unsure of how to tackle a technique or project you think might be dangerous, get assistance from someone who does know.

A dual-cartridge respirator protects against toxic vapours, like those from oil-based paints and solvents, and against toxic particles, like asbestos or saw-dust from treated lumber. Correct use of the respirator can prevent serious lung damage and disease. Make sure to use a Canadian-approved respirator. Use proper filters in the respirator cartridges and replace them according to the manufacturer's directions.

TIPS:

When using an extension cord, tie it with a simple knot to the tool's power cord. Knotting the cords is especially helpful when you are working on a ladder.

❖❖❖❖❖❖❖❖❖❖❖❖

Flying wood chips can damage or shatter a light bulb or fluorescent tube. Protect the fixtures by covering them with metal window screening or wire mesh (NOT nylon mesh which is not durable enough, and may melt).

Three-slot grounded receptacles provide some protection against shock but for maximum safety use a GFCI (ground-fault circuit-interrupter) in conjunction with a grounded receptacle. GFCIs sense small changes in current flow, like those that occur during a short circuit, and shut off power before a serious shock can occur. GFCI devices include plug-in portable units (A) and GFCI extension cords (B).

Ventilation & Dust Control

You will want to keep your workshop free of sawdust and waste materials. You're more likely to have accidents in a cluttered, dirty workshop, and you'll probably misplace tools and spoil expensive material.

An average workshop can produce nearly 30 pounds of sawdust a year – and much more if you do a lot of woodworking. If sawdust builds up, it can clog tool motors and gears, create a fire hazard and spread through the rest of your house. Instead of sweeping, which can increase the levels of airborne dust, use a heavy-duty shop vacuum to remove sawdust and dirt. If you plan to produce large amounts of sawdust, consider a dust collection machine. Canadian law now requires, for example, that if anyone is employed in a workshop, the employer must have dust control methods in place.

You'll also want to keep your air free of harmful fumes from paints, varnishes, cleaning solutions, solvents and other products.

Ventilate your workshop so that harmful vapours and fine dust particles are blown out. A simple household fan placed in a window can do the job as well as a permanent exhaust fan. Make certain the fan is pushing stale air out – and that another window on the opposite side of the room is open to admit fresh air.

Trap dust by taping a furnace filter to the intake side of a window fan. Place the fan next to your work area. It will clean dust from the air when sanding or sawing. When the filter is dirty, simply vacuum and reuse it.

When you've got a messy, dusty job to do, limit the fallout by hanging sheets of plastic around the work area. Turn off the heating and air-conditioning systems to prevent them from carrying fine sawdust throughout the house.

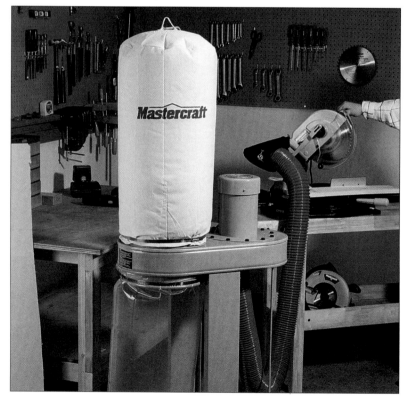

Some stationary tools, *such as power mitre saws and radial arm saws, have blade guard nipples that can be attached directly to a dust collection system on a shop vacuum hose. Before using the saw, turn on the vacuum to remove the sawdust as you work.*

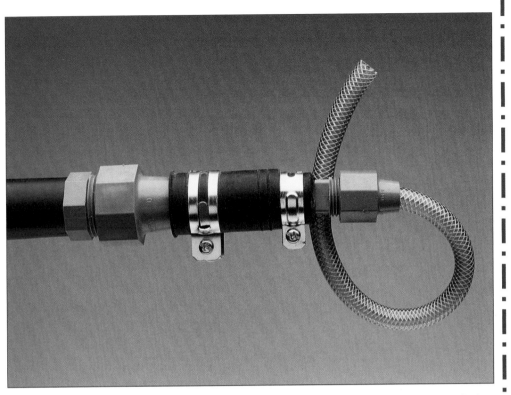

Hard-to-reach areas are difficult to clean with regular shop vacuum attachments. You can make a mini-vacuum attachment by using plastic plumbing tube and transition fittings, which are available at any plumbing supply store. Whenever it is needed, connect the attachment to your shop vacuum to clean crevices and tight areas, such as the space around a table saw motor.

Remove rust from metal surfaces with steel wool, using light machine oil as a lubricant. Wipe the rusty spot frequently with a clean rag to remove rust particles and steel wool fragments. Coat surfaces with light oil to prevent further rusting.

TIPS:

You can limit the amount of evaporation during paint-brush clean-up by using narrow plastic bottles that are just large enough to hold a brush. That way, you'll need a smaller volume of mineral spirits or liquid brush cleaners to cover the bristles.

❖❖❖❖❖❖❖❖❖❖

Place used mineral spirits in a sealed container until solid paint sediments settle out. Pour out the clear solvent for later use, then properly dispose of the residue.

❖❖❖❖❖❖❖❖❖❖

Basements, where many workshops are located, are notoriously damp places. High humidity can cause rust to form on tools and inside power tool motors, and it can hasten rot in wood. Use a dehumidifier to control dampness. You'll find a drier workshop is also a more pleasant place to spend time.

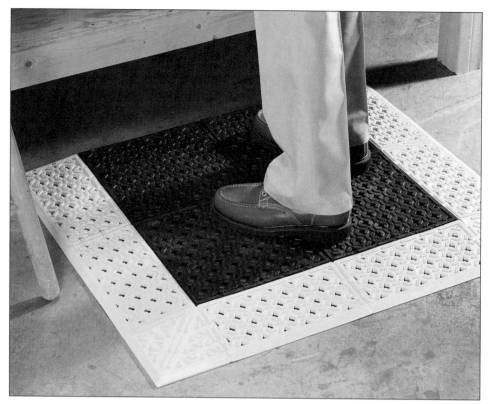

TIP:
To get rid of small amounts of paint, remove the lids and set the cans outdoors in a protected area where children and pets cannot reach them. Let the paint dry completely before throwing it away. Sand or sawdust can be used to absorb paint and speed up drying.

Safety & Comfort

Standing on a concrete workshop floor for long periods of time can tire leg and back muscles. Fatigue also contributes to shop accidents. Reduce muscle strain by laying a resilient rubber anti-fatigue mat on the floor in front of your work area (photo above). These mats are available at industrial tool supply stores. Or, use a piece of foam-backed carpeting. Wear sturdy shoes and equip your shop with a stool to further reduce fatigue.

Glove Help

Wear rubber gloves when working with solvent-based liquids. Some of these materials are absorbed through the skin and have been linked to serious health problems. Disposable rubber gloves are available at pharmacies and painting supply stores. Another benefit? Clean-up is a lot easier when wearing disposable gloves.

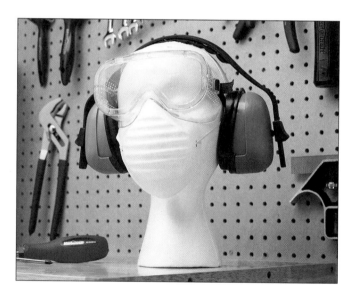

Protect Your Senses

Ear and eye protection is vitally important, but often overlooked in home workshops. If you are going to invest in a workshop, spend a few more dollars for safety glasses and hearing protection. To store these devices, use a rigid foam head (often sold to hold wigs or hats). Put the foam head in a conspicuous spot as a reminder to use the glasses, ear protection and any other safety devices.

Clean-up & Recycling

Check labels before disposing of a product and never pour hazardous liquids down the drain. If you do that, the material will eventually find its way into the area's drinking water supply. Products rated as environmental hazards carry one or more of the following terms: **Danger! Toxic, Harmful to Animals and Humans, Harmful Vapours, Poison, Flammable, Combustible, Corrosive, Explosive.**

If you have old power tools you don't use, donate them to vocational education centres for use in vocational training classes. Students can use the tools and your donation may be tax deductible.

Recycling companies in your area may buy or collect many types of scrap metal, including steel, iron, lead and copper from electrical wiring and plumbing pipes. Keep your scrap metal in a large box until you collect enough to recycle.

Mercury-free disposable batteries are less harmful to the environment than they once were, but it's still a good idea to keep them out of the household trash. Rechargeable tool batteries are a different story: they should never be thrown away in your house-

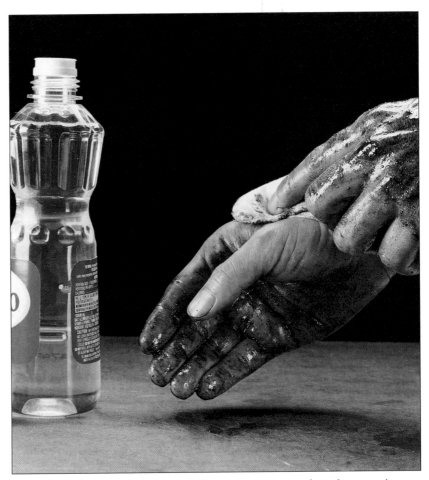

Hands soiled with oil or oil-based paints and stains can be cleaned with ordinary salad oil. Never use kerosene, mineral spirits or other solvents to wash the skin. These materials are skin irritants and can be absorbed through the skin, leading to increased health risks.

hold trash. Instead, call your municipal hazardous waste department for information on proper disposal sites, or return them to a location participating in the Charge Up to Recycle Program for rechargeable batteries.

TIP:

Combine several partial cans of leftover paint in one container to create a useable amount of paint for another project. Use paints that have similar colours so as to produce a tint that is not ghastly. You can also give leftover paint to church groups or civic organizations as long as the original product labels are not removed.

WORKSHOP TECHNIQUES

Having good tools, a well-organized workshop and fine materials is just part of what goes into making a successful project. Without the right techniques, you may find yourself disappointed by your handiwork.

This section will help you learn those techniques. You'll see dozens of tips and innovations that will help improve the quality of your workmanship.

Find the centre of a round or cylindrical workpiece with this jig (photo below), made from a framing square and a combination square. Simply clamp a combination square onto the framing square so that the 45° face of the combination square rests against one leg of the framing square. The top edge of the combination square should intersect the inside 90° corner of the framing square.

Place the jig over the workpiece (above) and draw pencil lines several times along the top edge of the combination square blade. The point where the lines intersect is the centre of the workpiece.

TIPS:

A piece of shelving standard makes a quick and versatile compass for producing accurate circle measurements. Drive a nail through the screw hole at one end of the standard and into the workpiece to mark the centre of the circle. Place the pencil in one of the slots so that the distance between the nail and the pencil is equal to the radius of the circle. Rotate the standard around the nail to draw the circle.

❖❖❖❖❖❖❖❖❖❖❖

The end hook on a tape measure has a small amount of play in it. For extremely accurate measurement, use the 1" mark as the starting point (and remember to subtract 1" from the final reading).

❖❖❖❖❖❖❖❖❖❖❖

Checking for square is crucial for building frames, boxes, cabinets, drawers and other projects where fit is important. Measure the diagonals of the workpiece. The diagonals should be identical if the workpiece is square.

❖❖❖❖❖❖❖❖❖❖❖

When cutting a series of identical workpieces, use only one piece as the pattern for laying out the other pieces. If you use each new piece to lay out the next piece, each new piece will be slightly larger than the last.

Dividing a board lengthwise into equal strips is difficult if the width of the board is not easily divisible by the number of parts. For example, imagine you need to cut a 5 3/4"-wide board into four equal strips. To do this job quickly and easily, position the 0" end of the ruler at one edge of the board. Angle the ruler across the board until the opposite edge of the board touches an inch measurement that is easily divisible by the number of parts. For the example shown, the ruler is angled until the 8" mark touches the edge of the board, and 8" divided by 4 equals 2". Mark the board at this interval along the ruler (A, B, C). Repeat this process at another location on the board and use the marks to draw parallel cutting lines on the board.

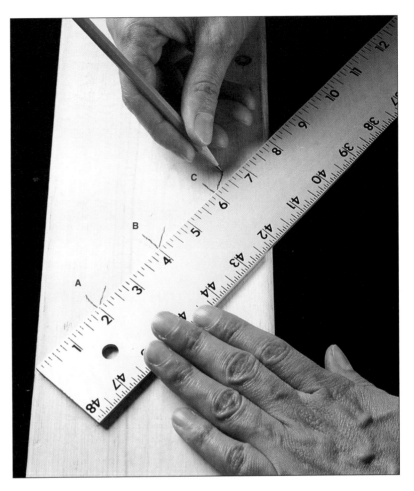

TIPS:

Taking an accurate inside measurement of a drawer or box is difficult because a tape measure will not fit into a corner and the measurement on the tape measure case that indicates its length is not accurate enough for precise work. For accurate measurements, position a square in the bottom of a workpiece, tight against the corner. Use a tape measure to measure from the opposite side of the workpiece to the tip of the square. Add the two lengths.

❖❖❖❖❖❖❖❖❖❖❖❖

To draw a line parallel to the edge of a board quickly, set the blade of a combination square to the desired distance. Position the flat side of the square against the edge of the board and place the pencil at the end of the blade. Pull the square and the pencil toward you to draw the line.

❖❖❖❖❖❖❖❖❖❖❖❖

When marking an identical series of measurements on many workpieces, save time and improve accuracy by creating a marking pattern, called a story pole. Make the story pole from a piece of scrap lumber, mark the measurements carefully on it and use it as a template for marking other pieces.

Measuring & Marking

You can find and mark the centre of your workpieces simply and quickly with this homemade marking jig (photo below). Construct it from 2x4 stock and 5/16" dowelling. On one side of the gauge shown here the dowels are centred 1" on either side of the pencil hole. Make sure the distance between each dowel and the pencil hole is equal. One side is used for marking centre on pieces up to 15/8" wide. The other side has the dowels centred 41/8" on each side of the pencil hole and is used on boards up to 73/4" wide. If you often use wider stock, you may wish to make a larger gauge.

Measure Diameters

Ever wonder how to easily measure the diameter of a round object? Make a simple gauge with a ruler and two squared blocks of wood. To find the diameter, place the workpiece between the two wood blocks and the ruler. The diameter measure is then easily read on the ruler. For the gauge to work properly, all six faces of each wood block must be perfectly squared.

Marking Slick Surfaces

Some materials, such as plastic, glass, ceramics and metal are difficult to mark. Solve the problem by using artist's tape to provide a surface on which to draw the pattern lines. Leave the tape in place until you are finished cutting. Artist's tape is easy to remove. It can be purchased at stationery stores or art supply stores.

Marking Protrusions

When you install panelling or drywall, cutting around protrusions such as electrical boxes can be difficult. Simplify the job by coating the edges of the box (or whatever is protruding) with carpenter's chalk. Press the back side of the panelling against the box to transfer the chalk outline. Then simply cut out the outline with a jigsaw.

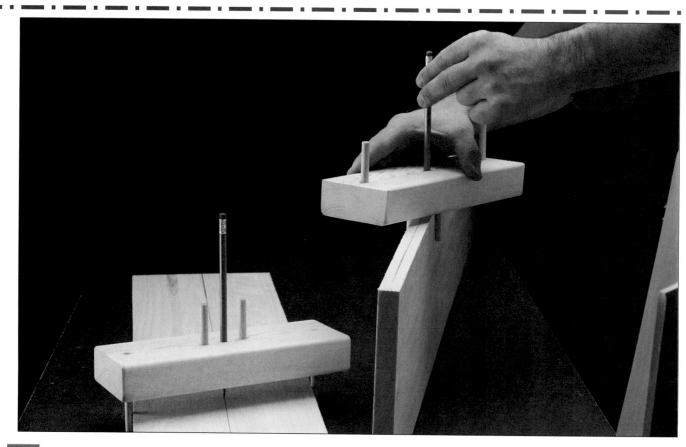

Clamping Techniques

Long workpieces balanced on a pair of sawhorses can be difficult to hold in place. Hold them securely with a bicycle inner tube. Slide the tube over the workpiece and use your foot to stretch the tube and hold the lumber in place while you work (photo below).

When gluing a wood strip to a flat surface, you can extend the reach of a C-clamp by using a short strip of scrap hardwood and a small wood block that is

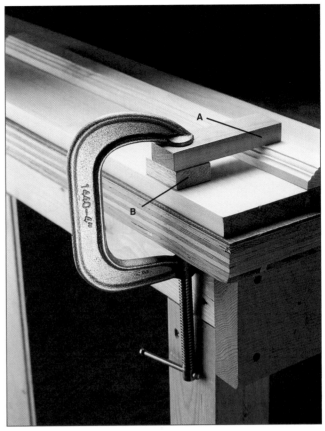

Hardwood strip (A), wood block (B).

the same thickness as the wood trim (photo above). Place the block close to the workpiece edge, then position the strip so it bridges the space between the block and the wood trim. Apply pressure to the strip with a C-clamp to hold the wood trim in place.

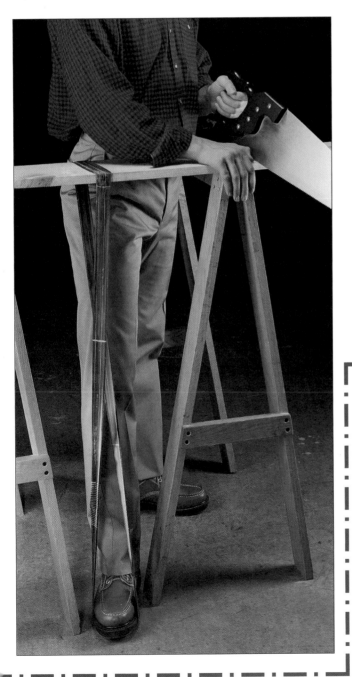

TIPS:

Use a bicycle inner tube to hold chair legs together while glued joints are drying. Loop the tube around the legs and use a strip of wood to twist the tube until it is stretched tight. Tie the strip to the inner tube to keep it from unwinding.

❖❖❖❖❖❖❖❖❖❖❖❖

Make a temporary soft clamp by slitting two old tennis balls and sliding them over the jaws of a locking pliers.

More Clamping Techniques

These simple door clamps made from scrap lumber (photo below) provide an easy way to hold doors in an upright position while installing locksets or hinges, or when planing or painting. The weight of the door causes the cross member of the clamp to bend slightly and force the uprights to grip the sides of the door.

Clamp Help

Get a better grip on smooth objects, such as metal pipes, by gluing emery-boards to the faces of vise jaws. The emery-boards can be removed easily with a chisel or paint scraper when they are no longer needed.

Distribute pressure evenly and prevent bowing when clamping small pieces of wood by using two sections of angle iron and a pair of C-clamps. Angle irons also prevent clamps from damaging the wood.

Hand power tools, such as drills and sanders, can be anchored temporarily to a workbench with handscrew clamps. The technique is good for sanding small workpieces. Clamp the tool securely so it does not move, but do not damage the tool by overtightening the clamp. A pad of soft foam or rubber under the handscrew jaw will help grip the tool while preventing damage to the tool casing.

Make simple, inexpensive band clamps by cutting rubber strips from inner tubes. Wrap the strips around the workpiece and knot the ends. For greater holding power, increase the number of bands tied around the piece.

Each clamp requires two 8"-long 2x4 uprights (A), a 1¹/2" x 16"-long plywood cross member (B), and two 2¹/2"-long 2x4 pieces (C). Join the pieces with carpenter's glue and wallboard screws. This design can be adapted to build clamps for holding framed storm windows or screens, plywood and other sheet goods.

Sanding & Finishing

Paint that has been stored *a long time can get lumpy. To guarantee a smooth finish, first mix the paint thoroughly and then strain it through an old nylon stocking, a piece of window screening or a piece of cheesecloth placed over the mouth of a coffee can.*

Sanding Belt Cleaner

Extend the life of sanding belts by cleaning them with an old tennis shoe that has a natural rubber sole. Turn the sander on and press the tennis shoe against the belt for a few seconds. Wood dust trapped between the abrasives on the sanding belt will cling to the rubber sole of the shoe.

Wallboard Sander

To create an excellent wallboard sander, simply wrap a piece of leftover window screening around a scrap piece of 2x4 and staple it into place. This sander works well for smoothing wallboard joints.

TIPS:

Paint the bottom edges of doors easily without removing them by using a scrap of carpet coated with paint. Painting the bottom of the doors seals the end grain, preventing the wood from absorbing moisture.

✦✦✦✦✦✦✦✦✦✦✦✦

If you need to hold a paint can for long periods of time, create a wire handle guard from an old garden hose. Slice a spiral cut in the hose, then fit the hose over the wire bucket handle.

✦✦✦✦✦✦✦✦✦✦✦✦

Painted workpieces can be propped up to dry on wallboard screws driven through small wood blocks. The screw points are very small and sharp and will not mar a freshly painted surface.

✦✦✦✦✦✦✦✦✦✦✦✦

Catch paint drips by hot-gluing a paper plate to the bottom of a paint can.

Index